FOR YOUTH MINISTRY

How to Use Music With Youth

Even If You're Musically Challenged

by Tim Gossett

ABINGDON PRESS

Nashville, Tennessee

About the Writer
Tim Gossett is director of youth ministries at First United Methodist Church in Plymouth, Michigan. Tim's four cats were glad that his guitar skills improved before he wrote this book; and his wife, Kathryn, was glad that the dining room table was finally cleared off.

Acknowledgments
Thanks to First UMC youth, Plymouth, Michigan; Ted Anderson, New York; Terry Gladstone and Ryan McNeill, Michigan; Joe Hesh, Pennsylvania; DiAnn L. Johnson, California

SKILLABILITIES FOR YOUTH WORKERS
How to Use Music With Youth—
Even If You're Musically Challenged
Volume 5

SKILLABILITIES FOR YOUTH WORKERS, Vol. 5
Copyright © 1997 by Abingdon Press. All rights reserved. No part of this work may be reproduced or transmitted in any form or by any means, electronic or mechanical, including photocopying or recording, or by any information storage or retrieval system, except as may be expressly permitted by the 1976 Copyright Act or in writing by the publisher. For some material, permission to photocopy is on the page. Requests for permission should be addressed to Abingdon Press, P.O. Box 801, 201 Eighth Avenue South, Nashville, TN 37202-0801. Printed in the United States of America.

Scripture quotations in this publication, unless otherwise indicated, are from the New Revised Standard Version Bible, copyright © 1989 by the Division of Christian Education of the National Council of Churches of Christ in the United States of America. Used by permission.

ISBN 0-687-08770-8

97 98 99 00 01 02 03 04 05 06—10 9 8 7 6 5 4 3 2 1

EDITORIAL AND DESIGN TEAM	**ADMINISTRATIVE TEAM**
Editor: Crystal A. Zinkiewicz	**Publisher:** Neil M. Alexander
Production Editor: Sheila K. Hewitt	**Vice President:** Harriett Jane Olson
Design Manager: Phillip D. Francis	**Executive Editor, Teaching and Study Resources:** Duane A. Ewers
Designer: Diana Maio	**Editor of Youth Resources:** M. Steven Games
Cover Design: Diana Maio & Phillip D. Francis	

CONTENTS

	page
WHY DO THIS? What's the benefit to youth, youth ministries, and churches?	4
WHAT'S THE WORD? Hear what the Bible says	11
WHAT'S THE CURRENT STATUS? Measure the interest. Note the resources. Pause to hear the music.	14
ADDING MUSIC TO YOUR RHYTHM 25 ways to tune up existing ministries	16
FROM THE TOP 15 ideas for using or developing musical gifts	37
PRACTICE MAKES PERFECT 10 "Musicabilities" for non-musical youth leaders	48
PLAYING BY THE RULES Copyrights and legal issues	58
SOUND BARRIERS AND OFF-BEAT PROBLEMS Harassment, talent, and content	63
MINI-WORKSHOP Perfect harmony—Making training easy	68
THE BIG PICTURE How does this SkillAbility fit in? What's next? Who's there to help?	71

WHY DO THIS?

Music is the thread that weaves our lives **together**.

Are You an Asset Builder?

Among the **40 key assets** that Search Institute has discovered that help youth to grow up healthy and whole is . .

CREATIVE ACTIVITIES Asset #17

Youth are involved 3 or more hours per week in lessons or practice in music, theater, or other arts.

© 1996 Search Institute, 700 South 3rd Street, Minneapolis, MN 55415, 612-376-8955. Used by permission.

Why Do This?

FastFacts . . .

Whose message are teens hearing?

- 93 percent of teens listen to radio each week.

- Radio is advertisers' most preferred way of reaching the teen market.

- Teens spend an average of 7 hours a week listening to radio and nearly 6 hours a week listening to CDs and tapes.

- 1 of every 5 pieces of stereo equipment is sold to a teen.

(All statistics are from *Billboard*, Feb. 17, 1996.)

Whose message are they buying?

"In some ways teens are better consumers than adults. Whatever money they have in their pockets they spend on themselves. They don't have other responsibilities."
—Marla Grossberg, Teenage Research Unlimited (*Restaurant Business*, May 1, 1996)

In 1995 the 12- to 19-year-old age group spent $109 billion—38 percent more than in 1990. Adolescents earn an average of $64 per week and spend 84 cents of every dollar. (*U.S. News & World Report*, July 1, 1996)

Columbia House and BMG Direct, two of the largest mail-order music clubs, recently turned their focus from Baby Boomers to Generation-Xers. Look for ads targeting Millenials in the near future.

Z Music Television, a Christian video version of MTV, reaches more than 20 million homes. (Source: Carolyn Davis, Z Music Television, Feb. 27, 1997)

Why Do This?

Why Do This?

A church's Grand Canyon may be the gap in musical tastes.

"Music is a language. It's learned, and many adults and most teenagers today 'speak' it without an accent. But there may be a problem. Over 70 percent of the human ear develops between the ages of three to seven. The sounds the ears hear in those early years are the native sounds that will not be erased by subsequent experiences. This means that some teachers, particularly in youth classes, do not speak the same musical language as their students. As we adults use music as a teaching tool, we must be aware of our prejudices and examine them carefully, if we do not wish to turn off our students to the possibility of developing their talents for use by God." (Marlene D. LeFever, *Creative Teaching Methods*, page 288)

But . . .

The **themes** remain
 the same—
  love, relationships,
 faith, meaning, joy, pain.

The **needs** haven't changed—
 expression,
  recreation, ritual,
 sound, connection.

What Are the Benefits?

Relevancy—Using music in youth ministry connects faith with culture and meaning with interests.

Literacy—Parents learn to understand their teens. Youth learn to critique contemporary media.

Skill Building—Music provides opportunities to learn a new skill or build on existing gifts.

Ministry—Youth touch peers and adults through leadership and lyrical faith-sharing.

Multisensory Learning—Emotions and intellect are aroused when various senses are tapped.

What's the Word?

"One who sings prays twice."

—Saint Ambrose

Music plays a key role throughout Scripture

The **Hebrews** used music to pass on their story (Exodus 15).

Music was an essential part of the **prophets'** training (1 Samuel 10:5; 2 Kings 3:15; 1 Chronicles 25:6).

Trained **singers** and **musicians** were a regular part of Temple services (2 Samuel 6:5; 1 Chronicles 15–16, 23:5, 25:1–6).

Solomon sang a song of love celebrating marriage (Song of Solomon 1–8).

Mary sang a song of praise to God for the conception of Jesus (Luke 1:46–55).

Jesus and his **disciples** sang a hymn (Matthew 26:30).

Paul and **Silas** sang hymns in prison (Acts 16:25).

We should sing to the Lord as a response to God's action in our lives (Ephesians 5:19–20; Colossians 3:16; James 5:13).

Psalm 150 (GOD'S WORD)

Hallelujah!

Praise God in his holy place.
Praise him in his mighty heavens.
Praise him for his mighty acts.
Praise him for his immense greatness.
Praise him with sounds from horns.
Praise him with harps and lyres.
Praise him with tambourines
and dancing.
Praise him with stringed
instruments and flutes.
Praise him with loud cymbals.
Praise him with crashing
cymbals.
Let everything that breathes
praise the Lord!

Hallelujah!

GOD'S WORD is a copyrighted work of God's Word to the Nations Bible Society. Quotations are used by permission. Copyright © 1995 by God's Word to the Nations Bible Society. All rights reserved.

What's the Word?

What's the Current Status?

One Verse at a Time

Measure the Interest

How many of your youth are currently involved in musical activities at school, in church, or on their own? What percentage of your youth actively listen to Christian music? Have previous music-related events and programs been well received by the youth? Gather information about your youth and their current musical interests and abilities.

Note the Resources

Are there adult musicians in your church who would enjoy the opportunity to work with youth? Ask your choir members, choir director, organist, and others how they could help you. Take stock of your physical and financial resources: VCRs, boom boxes, video cameras, local library CD and magazine collections, and so forth.

Pause to Hear the Music

You don't have to like it, but it's crucial to begin learning about the music that your youth enjoy and listen to regularly. Survey their interests.

Check out current music magazines at the library and bookstore. Spend time every week listening to various radio stations (especially top-10 or top-40 countdown programs). Listen for trends in the songs' themes—anger, sex, spirituality, and so forth.

Adding Music To Your Rhythm

25 Ways to Tune Up Existing Ministries

1 ADD MUSIC TO BIBLE STUDIES

Open or close your Bible study with recorded music. Select a song that fits the theme of the Bible study, then play it for the group. Display the lyrics on an overhead projector a line at a time (rather than all at once) as the song is played. (See "Playing by the Rules," page 58.)

2 LOOK UP THE MEANING

Many Christian songs are loosely or directly based on Scriptures. Look through the music credits on CD or cassette covers for Scripture references. Have youth look them up to shed light on a song's meaning.

3 CONSIDER THE COST

Students can evaluate their own listening and purchasing habits during Bible studies of stewardship, renewing one's mind, and focusing on God. Ask questions like, "How do your musical spending habits reflect your spiritual beliefs?" "When you purchase an artist's music, you are saying that you support what the artist says and does and how he or she lives his or her life. What kind of lifestyle do you want to support?"

4 USE SONGS TO INTERPRET SCRIPTURE

During a group Bible study of a particular passage, ask the youth to bring to the next class songs of any kind that describe the meaning of that Scripture. Play the songs and explore how the cultural and gospel messages connect.

5 REFLECT ON THEOLOGICAL IMAGES

Tell your group to bring CDs to the next class. Choose a theological theme to study that day, such as love, evil, sin, grace, sex; then find three or four contemporary Christian music (CCM) songs that illustrate that theme.

When the class meets again, tell the youth the theme and have them find songs on their CDs that relate. The only ground rule is that the words must be easily understandable or be available in print, such as in the liner notes. Listen to a selection, then reflect on the message about the theme in the song.

Finally, play the CCM songs you brought. Reflect, compare, and draw conclusions together. You may wish to bring in additional material, such as profiles of individuals or relevant Scripture passages to supplement the discussion of the theme.

6 MEMORIZE WITH SONGS

Music can be an effective aid to Scripture memorization. Praise and worship songs, for example, are often taken directly from modern translations of the Bible. Sing some of these songs regularly at your youth events, reminding youth where the words of the song originated. Students may even write their own simple tunes to help them memorize their favorite verses.

Adding Music to Your Rhythm

Adding Music

7 PRAY TO MUSIC

Use soft jazz or meditative music as quiet background sound for your prayer sessions, especially when doing guided meditations with youth. The music will help youth focus and relax during prayer times.

8 HOLD COFFEEHOUSE POETRY SESSIONS

Many coffeehouses feature poets who read their works to a musical accompaniment. Since many music lyrics are essentially a contemporary form of poetry, this is a natural combination. Get your teenage poets to bring their poetry and experiment with various types of background accompaniment.

9 UNCOVER HIDDEN EMOTIONS

Since lyrics often express human emotions in powerful ways, music is a powerful master key that can unlock the emotional lives of your youth.

Ask a youth to tell you the titles of three songs:

- one that describes his or her emotional state about two years ago,

- one that expresses his or her emotions during the last year, and

- one that sums up how he or she is feeling right now.

Track down those songs and listen to them very carefully. You'll gain insights into what youth really think about themselves; and you'll have a great discussion starter for one-on-one, confidential, in-depth conversations.

Adding Music to Your Rhythm

Adding Music

10 STOP THE MUSIC!

Have everyone sing a song that your group knows well; but after a stanza or two, interrupt your song leaders and stop the music. The youth will be in shock. Ask a question about the stanza, such as:

- "How have you experienced this in your life?" or

- "When is it hardest for you to believe that?"

Let the youth and leaders discuss that for a moment, then continue with the rest of the song. By doing this occasionally, you'll find that teens will think about the words more carefully, particularly those of songs they've sung together a hundred times.

Another possibility
Between stanzas, have everyone get up and speak to another person whom he or she needs to encourage, to ask for forgiveness of, to express appreciation for, and so forth.

11 ATTEND A CONCERT

Vary your usual programming by attending a Christian concert in your area. Not sure where concerts are being held? Check publications like *CCM* and *Christian Happenings*, cover-notes of the latest CDs, or Christian book stores for concert listings.

12 EXTEND THE EXPERIENCE

Hold a pre-concert party before you all pile into the church van for the drive to the concert. The activities could include artist trivia contests, name-the-tune games, videos, pizza while listening to the artist's CDs, and other events. Scheduling this special party also gives those who cannot go to the concert itself a chance to take part in the fun.

Be sure that every vehicle has tapes or CDs of Christian artists to listen to during the drive. Provide lyric sheets (and a flashlight, if driving at night) to passengers who are unfamiliar with the words to the songs. (See "Playing by the Rules," page 58.)

13 SUPPORT MUSIC IN THE BUDGET

Consider setting aside part of your youth budget to reduce the cost of concert tickets. Alternatively, let youth earn credits toward ticket costs during your youth ministry fundraisers. Buy an extra ticket or two for a youth who decides at the last minute to go, or offer tickets for free to marginally active or unchurched youth. Also use extra tickets as give-aways and prizes at your other youth events.

14 BRING IN THE BAND

Many new artists can be booked for just a few hundred dollars, so consider bringing a local band (future star?) to your church for a concert. The youth will benefit from the experience of being able to meet the musicians personally, plus they may be able to help as stage crew members. Invite other local and district churches to your event at least two months ahead of time, and you'll find that you have a larger turnout without spending a lot of money on advertising. Your concert could also be a fundraiser, an evangelistic event, or the entertainment during an all-church potluck.

Adding Music

15 BRING IN THE BAND "LITE"

Call booking agents (many are listed in *Group* and *Youthworker Journal*) to see if any of their artists will be near your area in the future. Ask if it would be possible to bring them to your church youth group meeting just to talk with youth about their music. If you're lucky, you may get them to agree to an acoustic mini-concert to boot! Or arrange through their booking agent a phone (or online) interview with the artists. All you'll be out is the cost of a long-distance phone call and a speaker phone.

16 ATTEND A FESTIVAL

Plan to attend one of the annual Christian music festivals, such as Creation, Cornerstone, or ICHTHUS. These two- to four-day events draw huge crowds, in part because they are a tremendous value. Some of them have multiple concerts being performed at the same time, which gives your youth several musical options. You'll also be likely to hear some lesser-known bands who may well become next year's big stars.

Most of the festivals feature well-known youth speakers during the mornings and afternoons. Plan to camp out at the site of the event for a small additional fee, bring lots of food with you, and get set for a few days of incredible fun! Information about these events is available online and through many of the popular Christian music and leadership magazines.

Adding Music

17 REVISIT "JESUS LOVES ME"

Almost everyone knows the first stanza to the song "Jesus Loves Me," but did you know that at least a dozen other stanzas exist? Search old hymnals and song books for other stanzas. Read through the lyrics a stanza at a time and consider the theological concepts represented in that stanza. What images of God do the stanzas contain? What view of Jesus do they present? Are the images appropriate for children to hear? Do our theological beliefs change over time, as we grow older and as society changes?

Jesus Loves Me

Jesus loves me, this I know,
For the flowers tell me so,
Tell me by their fragrance sweet,
Lying all around our feet.

Chorus: Yes, Jesus loves me;
Yes Jesus loves me;
Yes, Jesus loves me;
The Bible tells me so.

Jesus loves me, this I know,
For the sunbeams tell me so,
Tell me by their gladsome light,
Shining clear from morn to night.

(Repeat Chorus.)

18 STUDY THE HYMNAL WITH A YOUTHFUL EYE

Hymns often lose their power for certain generations, because the words seem sexist ("Faith of Our Fathers"), militaristic ("Onward Christian Soldiers"), or foreign ("There Is a Balm in Gilead").

Page through the hymnal and note the songs that you remember singing as a youth but that are no longer meaningful to you. Ask youth to list their favorite and least-favorite hymns, and provide this list to your pastor or worship committee.

Adding Music

19 HYMNAL NIGHT—SERIOUSLY?

Bring your church hymnal to life for your teens by holding a special Hymnal Fest at youth group. Here are a few possibilities to get you started:

- Many hymn writers have their own special style and theological biases. Look at several hymns by Charles Wesley, Brian Wren, Fanny Crosby, or other writers who have multiple hymns in your hymnal. What do their songs have in common?

- If your church still has copies of an older hymnal, have youth see what songs are missing from newer versions. What reasons can they suggest for why certain songs were not included?

- Hold a hymn sing-off. Divide the group into two teams, then call out a word common to many hymns (Jesus, heart, Lord). Teams get 20–30 seconds to find a hymn with that word in it and then sing a phrase from that hymn. Teams alternate singing until one team runs out of time. The team that sings last gets a point.

- Get a book such as *The Companion to The United Methodist Hymnal*, by Carlton Young (Abingdon Press), or *101 Hymn Stories*, by Kenneth W. Osbeck (Kregel Publications), to learn about the history of songs. Summarize the story of a particular song for youth and then sing the song together. How does knowing the history of the song enhance your enjoyment or understanding of it? What experiences in your life were so meaningful that you could have written an entire hymn describing them? Youth who have musical or poetic abilities might enjoy trying to write their own hymn lyrics based on their own stories.

- Hymnals often have many unusual features not found in popular song books, like liturgies, prayers, worship services, special indexes, and so forth. Invite the pastor to guide the youth group through some of these worship aids. Also invite your music director to explain how to use some of the tools that aid worship planners. Try singing songs with the same meter to different tunes.

- Borrow hymnals from several area churches. In small groups, youth can explore the differences.

Adding Music to Your Rhythm

Adding Music

20 WRITE A PRIZE-WINNING SONG

Hymn contests are often held by church districts, workshops, conferences, publishers; and many times the rules specify that lyrics should be written to an existing tune in the public domain

Youth can work in small groups to write rough drafts of new lyrics. Tell them not to worry about getting every beat and rhythm exactly right the first time through—just get the ideas down that they'd like to express, along with some good phrases and rhymes.

Then ask students who are gifted in music to polish the lyrics, refining them and making sure they fit the meter of the song. Who knows? They could win a cash prize for your youth group!

21 USE THE INTERNET

Surf the web (or get your Internet-savvy youth to do it for you!) for artist information, song chords, lyrics, and music-related graphics. Many musicians and music companies have their own Web sites. Publish the best ones in your church newsletters. (See "Playing by the Rules," page 58.)

Adding Music

22 HOLD A CONTEST

Is your group passionately into contemporary Christian music? Hold a "Name the Tune" competition some evening, with gift certificates from the local Christian music store as prizes.

23 MAKE A VIDEO

Create your own Christian music videos. Let youth pick a contemporary Christian song they like, then provide a video camera or two and let them use their creativity. Be sure to become familiar with copyright restrictions (see "Playing by the Rules," page 58).

24 START A MUSIC LIBRARY

Form a music and video club in your youth group. Ask for donations of money and music, charge a small membership fee, buy some new CDs, set some membership rules, and you're ready to go!

Also, contact Interlinc Music Service at 800-725-3300 for information on "Youth Leaders Only." You can receive CDs/cassettes, videos, Bible studies, and artist posters. The approximate costs are $7.00 per CD or $3.00 per cassette.

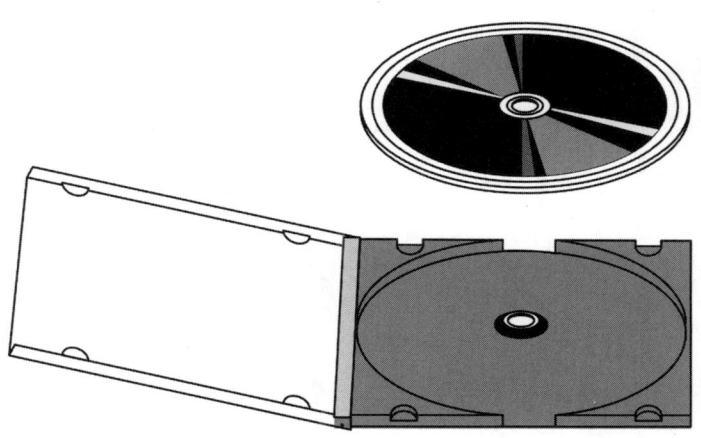

25 CREATE A REASON TO PARTY

Hold a Dove Awards Party during April of each year. Gather people together at a home with a big-screen TV and cable (check local listings or *CCM* magazine for time and date) and celebrate together the best that Christian music has to offer. Trivia contests, guess-the-winner games, and debates about anything—from who really should have won to whether Christians should give such awards—can round out the evening.

15 Ideas for Letting Youth Use and Develop Musical Gifts

1 CONNECTION THROUGH LESSONS

Are there any adults who play instruments or who are talented vocalists in your congregation? Ask them if they would be willing to offer free or low-cost lessons to youth, especially those who are just beginning to learn an instrument. Not only will youth gain valuable attention to their new skill, they'll build a relationship with a mentor.

2 SING WITH YOUR HANDS

Many youth enjoy learning sign language, and music becomes more beautiful—and visual—when the words are signed. Local schools, colleges, and social service agencies might be able to connect you to someone who could teach a few youth some basic sign language. Then they can share their new gift with the youth group or the whole congregation.

3 CONNECT CHILDREN AND YOUTH

Encourage your musical youth to lead songs during children's church or Sunday school. This serves a dual purpose: You'll give youth a chance to use their skills and be mentors to the children while you teach children songs they'll want to sing in youth group when they become teens.

4 GET 'EM ON THE WORSHIP CALENDAR

Commitment to a youth choir tends to increase with the frequency of performances in worship. Schedule Sundays with the music director (shoot for a minimum of once a month) and give the dates to the youth well in advance.

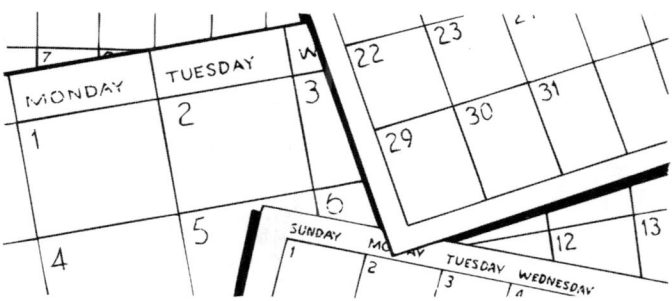

5 LET 'EM SHINE

Talent shows are marvelous opportunities for youth to show off their skills. Plus the shows give you a chance to see adults share musical gifts you didn't know they had. Build an all-church talent show into your annual schedule and get ready for a wonderfully entertaining event!

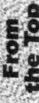

6 INVITE! INVITE! INVITE!

Regularly invite youth to participate in the musical life of the church at all levels—choirs, special cantatas, hymn selection, preludes, bell choirs, and so forth. Provide training for youth to be sound technicians; many will jump at the chance to work with microphones and other sound equipment.

7 WRITE A SONG

Encourage youth to write praise lyrics and other simple songs, even if they are able only to write the words. Put the words to a simple tune (perhaps a choir member or even a music major at a local college could do this). Then sing the song at youth events. The words may not win a Grammy, but they will reflect the concerns of your youth and make your teenage writer feel truly special.

8 GIVE EVERYONE AN OPPORTUNITY

Remember that youth have differing gifts. Those who sing or play the music are often given many outlets for their talents, while those who can do something to or with the music are overlooked.

- Encourage dancers to develop liturgical dances or simple moves for congregations to do during praise choruses.

- Ask the group photographer to put a slide show to music for use in a worship service.

- Have artists apply their creativity to paint a mural or make a banner based on a song lyric.

- Athletes and gymnasts might like to develop a Christian music aerobics class. Even martial arts could be choreographed to music.

When talent and music are combined, the result is meaningful ministry!

9 DEVELOP YOUTH ACCOMPANISTS

Accompanying a choir is a special skill that differs considerably from playing solo pieces. Ask your choir director if some of your talented youth pianists could accompany a song on occasion. Also, adding piano to your regular organ accompaniment of hymns will add a special dimension to their sound.

10 SING UNDER THE STARS

Send youth to church-related summer camps. Your teens will come back with a wealth of new songs. Some church camps have an emphasis on creative and performing arts. If your conference doesn't yet offer a music camp, ask camping staff to start one next year.

11 STRETCH YOUTH CHOIR BOUNDARIES

If your youth choir sings only on occasion at your church, challenge them to try something new. Learn a youth musical (Abingdon Music, 800-672-1789) or write your own, using songs from a variety of sources (see "Playing by the Rules," page 58). Then invite other youth groups to see it.

12 VISIT EAGER AUDIENCES

Retirement centers are always interested in having youth share their musical abilities with them. The residents would love a chance to hear youth sing or play their instruments. An old-fashioned hymn singing is always a sure-fire hit.

13 TAKE A TOUR

Take your youth choir on a tour to other churches, even if you think your group is not good enough. Reverend David Gladstone, a youth choir director, says, "Touring builds community; community builds skill." (From "Youth Choir Tours," *News Notes*, May 1988, page 3)

- You'll give the youth a tremendous experience in Christian living.

- You'll get youth out of their comfort zone and into other surroundings.

- You'll spread Christ's message in a new and powerful way.

From the Top

14 HAVE ANY REQUESTS?

Let youth choose the music for your group sing-alongs when possible. Designate a place where youth may write song requests for the next meeting. Then work with your music leadership team to put the songs in an order, to learn unfamiliar songs, and to practice each one. In this way, you'll be sure to sing songs the youth like and know while giving everyone a chance to suggest the new songs they'd like to learn.

15 BUILD A MUSIC RESOURCE FILE

Work with one or two of your well-organized or shy youth to build a music resource file cabinet. Gather overheads, articles about various groups or artists, new ideas from youth ministry magazines, and so forth; then organize and store them in an accessible file cabinet. Encourage others to use the material.

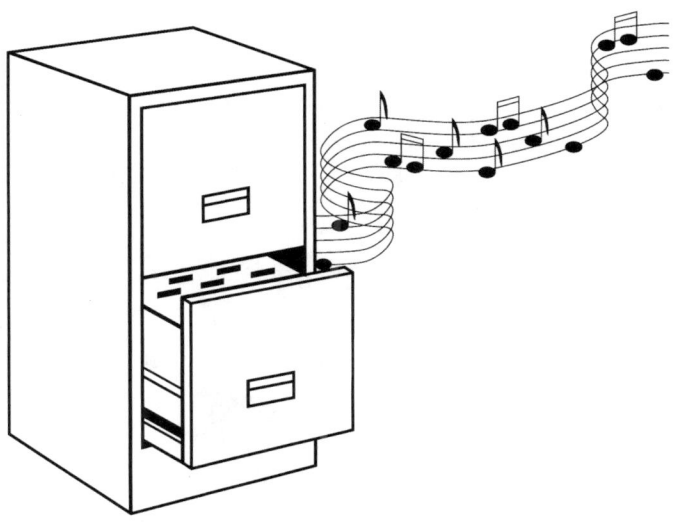

From the Top

PRACTICE MAKES PERFECT

10 "Musicabilities" for Non-Musical Youth Leaders

You say you have no musical ability beyond pushing the play button on the CD player? Your only knowledge of "fretting" has nothing to do with guitars? Don't worry—there are still many ways for you to bring music into your group.

1 TAP IN TO THE MOST VALUABLE RESOURCE: YOUR YOUTH

Youth who play an instrument or who sing well are not only potential music leaders; they're teens who will greatly benefit from the chance to be seen by their peers as skilled, competent people who are important to the group. Let the abilities of the musicians guide where you begin; but keep encouraging your music leaders to develop new skills, new songs, and new ministries.

Also, ask your youth if they have friends who play the piano, guitar, or drums well. These youth may jump at the chance to creatively use their skills. Otherwise they may never step foot into your church.

Practice Makes Perfect

2 USE A BACKUP BAND THAT ALWAYS SOUNDS GREAT

Use song tracks for your group singing. Available at Christian music stores, these tapes and CDs feature the latest hit songs recorded both with and without lyrics. Some collections even come with overhead masters or CD-ROM technology that allows you to display the lyrics. Get a small group together to learn the songs, then have them lead the singing for your whole group.

3 BRING OUT THE ELVIS IN THEM

Secular and Christian karaoke tapes are a fun resource that anyone can use. Not only are they great to get groups singing during "down times" at retreats and lock-ins, you can work together to rewrite secular lyrics to be more Christian-friendly. Cokesbury's *Youth! Praise 3: Jesus Is the Rock* (800-672-1789) and Carport Sound (903-832-4080) are two sources for karaoke tapes.

4 TRY THE LATEST TECHNOLOGY

A hot new option is to use MIDI technology as background music for your group. These special computer files contain words and music for a song, and they allow you to choose the instrumentation setup and even the key signature for a particular song. Each voice part can be listened to individually for practice purposes. In essence, your computer (or special MIDI-compatible portable stereo) becomes the music teacher and accompanist!

Talk to your local professional music store to learn more about MIDI technology or try AdventSource (800-328-0525) to get more information about their Step by Step praise team system for youth groups.

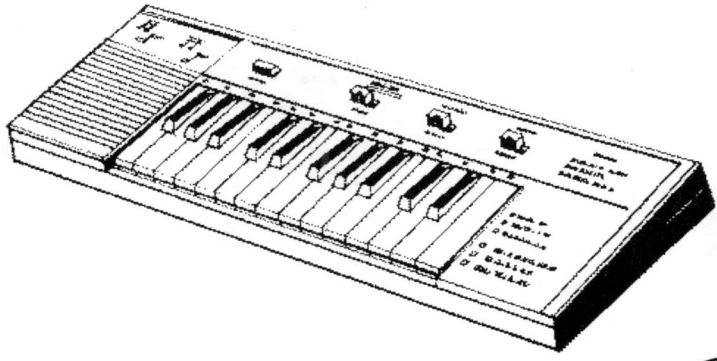

5 IT'S AS SIMPLE AS IT GETS

Don't be afraid to have your group sing a capella (without musical accompaniment). Crazy song sessions in the church van and soft reflective worship services lend themselves well to this style of singing—and nobody will care if you can't sing like Amy Grant.

Clapping and simple rhythm instruments (sticks, pencils, small drums) can provide a little-talent-required form of accompaniment.

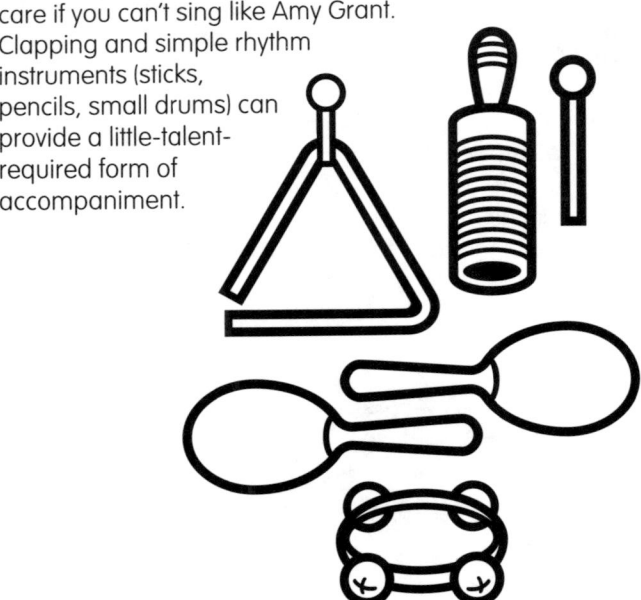

How to Use Music With Youth

6 ASSUME THAT THEY DON'T KNOW THE WORDS

There's little guarantee that youth, especially guests and those new to Christianity, know the lyrics to even the most popular Christian songs. Always provide the lyrics or teach a song as if no one has heard it before. Otherwise, you risk giving someone the impression that they are excluded from your group.

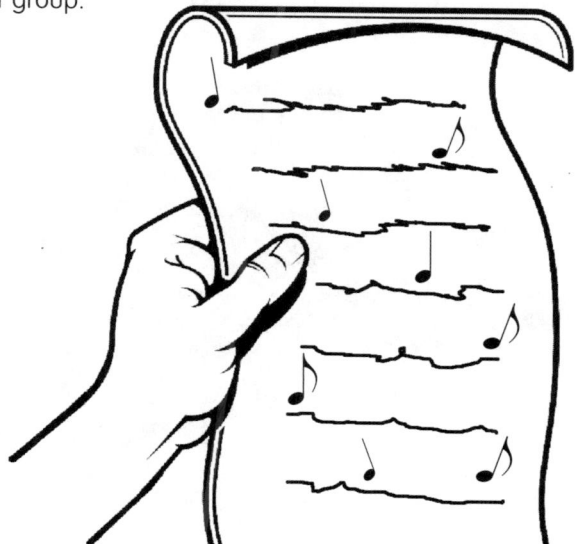

Practice Makes Perfect

Practice Makes Perfect

7 HESITATION BREEDS FORGETFULNESS

Ever heard a song you really liked but couldn't remember later? Chances are you'd still know the words if you had immediately pursued them. Whenever you hear a song you like—especially if your youth like it too—find out from the song leader or radio station the source for that song. Then practice it a few more times to make sure you can recall it later.

Practice Makes Perfect

8 TUNE IN TO CAR TUNES

Teens seem to instinctively turn on their favorite station in the church van or your car, but not everyone wants to hear the same music on those long trips. What can you do?

- Encourage your student leadership team to set some rules about music during road trips.
- Ask youth to make and bring their own tapes of their favorite songs.
- Let the person riding in front control the music and listen to no more than three songs from any CD or tape.
- Use the ride as an opportunity to talk about the lyrics in secular music. Try asking, "What do you think this song is about?" or "I can't quite make out all the words. What are they saying?"

Practice Makes Perfect

9 HANG OUT WITH MUSICIANS

Get to know some of the musicians who play in local bands. They'll help you understand the contemporary music scene and provide you with valuable information about youth culture, sound equipment, and so forth. Plus they may be musicians who could start (or be fill-ins for) your church praise team.

Also, visit youth groups in your area who are already doing great praise and worship with youth. They'll be glad to share their insights about what works with youth.

10 LEARN THE GUITAR . . . OR THE YOTAR

Thinking about learning an instrument but not sure whether to focus on piano or guitar? Go with the guitar—it's easier, cheaper, and much more transportable. Practice a half-hour a day for a year and you'll definitely be able to lead a sing-along.

Better yet, get a Yotar. This specially designed 12-string guitar has a bigger sound and simpler finger arrangements, so it's even easier to learn. (The Yotar is available from Songs & Creations, 800-227-2188.)

PLAYING BY THE RULES

Rules to Remember

1. Any time you're making a copy of a song—whether it's from print, audio, or video—**you need permission.**

2. When in doubt about Rule 1, ask anyway.

Copyright Q&A

Q Why should I bother to get permission? It's such a hassle, and it squashes creativity.

A **First, because it is the legal thing to do.** To put it simply, copying music illegally is theft. Many churches have been taken to court for illegally copying music.

Second, it is the ethical thing to do. Musicians who don't sell music don't make money. By illegally copying music, you deprive them of their livelihood and ability to create new music in the future.

Third, by doing so you teach your youth that just because something is possible (like copying a friend's CD) does not mean that it's right.

Playing by the Rules

Q I want to make overheads of some songs to sing at youth group. Whom do I contact?

A Start by contacting Christian Copyright Licensing, Inc. (CCLI), at 800-257-2230. It provides copyright privileges for thousands of songs—more than you'll ever need. The cost is based on your church size. If CCLI cannot provide you with permission, try contacting the publisher or individual songwriter.

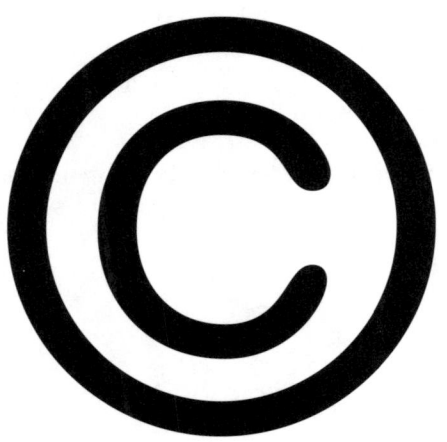

Playing by the Rules

Q **We want to make our own Christian music video, using a track from our favorite CD. Do we need permission?**

A Yes, two kinds: 1) Each song (words and music) has a copyright holder; and 2) the copyright of the recording itself is held by the music company. Contact the copyright administrator from the company, giving them as much information as possible about how you will be using the song. Permission may take anywhere from two to six weeks, so plan ahead. Fax your requests whenever possible to speed the response time.

You may be charged a modest fee, depending on how you will be using the song. If you're not going to be selling the video but will be giving the tape away as a gift, be sure to ask if they'll waive the fee.

Contact the Gospel Music Association (GMA) at 615-242-0303 for the phone numbers and addresses of most Christian musicians and music companies.

Playing by the Rules

Playing by the Rules

 Can we show videos taped from MTV and Z Music Television during a lock-in?

The copyright for MTV videos is held by the individual record label, which you should contact for permission to use a taped video for discussion purposes. You may wish to talk with parents before using MTV videos; some parents may object to the content.

Z Music Television is glad to have you show their videos in your youth group. Also, Christian music videos can be purchased from your local Christian book and music store, directly from WORD Music, or from Interlinc Music Service.

 **We'd like to videotape a special concert by our praise and worship band. Is this allowed?**

 Assuming, of course, that the songs weren't written by your group, you should check with the copyright holders and provide them with the details of what songs you wish to record and how the videotape will be used.

Sound Barriers and Off-Beat Problems

Here are some of the common complaints you may hear as you work to tie music and youth ministry together and suggestions of how you might respond:

"But our choir won't sound as good if we invite kids to be in it!"

Most youth don't sing very loud, so there's a good chance the quality of the sound won't change a bit. Teens who are willing to share their skills and sing music that they may not even like should be celebrated not reprimanded.

Sound Barriers

"But their music is so loud!"

Most people dislike the music of the generation before and after them, so don't expect that adults will enjoy (or understand) the music that youth like. However, adults will appreciate hearing how the music has a positive impact on youth. Let youth give testimony to how contemporary Christian music has changed their lives in some way and has strengthened their spiritual journey.

"But we'll look stupid if we do that!"

Most teens feel self-conscious about their bodies, and they may regard movements to songs as both ridiculous and embarrassing. Try attending a bigger event like a conference or camp where youth do motions to the songs. The positive peer pressure will break down the barriers, and teens will come home more willing to do the motions.

Above all, never embarrass your youth. Not everyone will like your style of music, your musical selections, or your silly movements.

Encourage —**never force**— youth to participate.

Sound Barriers and Off-Beat Problems

Sound Barriers

"You're not bringing guitars and drums into this worship service!"

Change always disrupts the current way of thinking, so realize that it will probably be easier to add a new contemporary worship service than to change the existing one. However, if you do wish to bring "those instruments" into traditional worship, do it gradually. For example, add drums to a well-known song from the hymnal and check out the reaction. Either people will come around to accepting it, or they'll make it clear that under no circumstances are drums, guitars, and so forth allowable.

"That's not appropriate in church!"

Jesus didn't live in a vacuum; he was always on the cutting edge in his teaching style and lessons. The church cannot afford to do less. While some songs are obviously inappropriate for certain settings, the church must explore ways to link faith and culture.

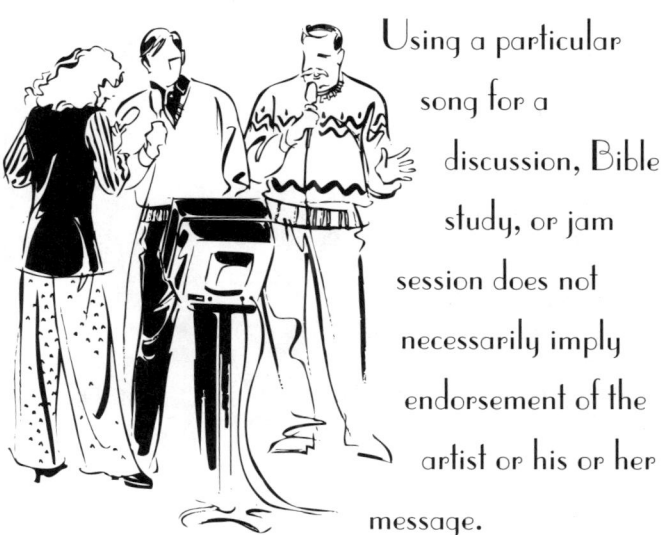

Using a particular song for a discussion, Bible study, or jam session does not necessarily imply endorsement of the artist or his or her message.

Mini-Workshop

FOR LEADERS

minutes

- PREPARATION
  - —Ask each participant to bring 10 favorite CDs or tapes.
  - —Borrow CDs, tapes, and music magazines from youth.

- GATHERING 5–10
  - —Play Christian CDs or videos as background music.

- SING YOUR PRAISE 5–10
  - —Sing a few well-known songs or hymns, plus teach a new song.
  - —Participants may lead, accompany, and so forth, depending on skills.

- BIBLE STUDY/DEVOTION (pages 11–13) 10–15
  - —Use as your theme a song based on a psalm, such as "Praise Ye the Lord," by Petra, or "40," by U2.

	minutes

Mini-Workshop

- ADDING MUSIC TO YOUR RHYTHM (pages 16–36) 5–10
  - Why Do This? (page 5–11)
  - Browse current CDs and magazines.

- A LOOK AT OUR ORCHESTRA (pages 14–15) 10–15
  - What's the Current Status?
  - Have participants brainstorm suggestions, then fill in anything they forgot.

- WHAT PART CAN YOU PLAY? (pages 48–57) 15–20
  - Split the group into smaller groups of 2 or 3. Provide Bibles, CDs/tapes, paper, and so forth.
  - Each group receives instructions for one idea from Adding Music to Your Rhythm (especially Ideas 1, 2, 4, 5) or From the Top (role play Ideas 6 or 8; try Idea 7).

- PRACTICE THE SKILLS 20–30
  - Each group micro-teaches their mini-lesson.
  - Debrief the experience and how it relates to your youth.

- PLAYING BY THE RULES (pages 58–62) 5–10
  - Basic rules
  - Common scenarios
  - Where to go for permission

- CLOSING 5–10
  - Read Psalm 150.
  - Sing another song or two.

Mini-Workshop

Coda: Resources

Books
- The Art of Relaxed Song Leading, by Yohann Anderson (Songs and Creations, 800-227-2188)
- Music Worth Talking About, by Patty and Tim Atkins (Baker Books, 1995)
- Understanding Today's Youth Culture, by Walt Mueller (Tyndale House Publishers, Inc., 1994)
- Dancing in the Dark, by Quentin J. Schultze, et al. (Wm. B. Eerdmans, 1991).

Youth Musicals
- Youth! Praise 3: Jesus Is the Rock (800-672-1789)
- Lost and Found (800-672-1789)
- Back to Bethlehem (800-672-1789)

Music
- New music sources include Hosanna Music (800-877-4443); Maranatha (800-444-4012); Saddleback Praises (800-458-BSSB); Brentwood Music (800-333-9000); In His Image (800-452-9571); Wellsprings Unlimited, Inc. (612-890-3863).
- Songs, published by Songs and Creations (800-227-2188)

Recorded Music Sources
- Abingdon Music (800-672-1789)
- Interlinc Music Service (800-725-3300)
- Youth Leaders Only (affordable quarterly music subscription)
- Rad Rockers (313-439-7029). www.radrockers.com
- True Tunes (630-665-3866). www.truetunes.com

THE BIG PICTURE

Working with youth is a little like putting together a jigsaw puzzle: It helps to have a picture of what it's supposed to look like! (See page 73.)

In effective youth ministry **vision** is central.

Seven major elements contribute to realizing that vision. The more of them that are developed and in place, the better.

Youth ministry planners in individual churches can develop each of those areas **their own way**, according to their congregation's particular resources, gifts, and priorities and the needs of their youth.

The Big Picture

How does this SkillAbility fit in this big picture? Here are just a few of the ways. By using ideas in this book, not only do you bring music into the church's vocabulary for reaching young people's souls, you also

- give them language and melody for **EXPERIENCES** of loving God

- honor youth with your **PERSPECTIVE** of them as partners and leaders with gifts, which they can share with others

- build into your **STRUCTURE** places and opportunities to connect youth to one another, to the community of faith, and to God

- send youth into the **COMMUNITY** to witness through music to the love of God for each of us

YOUTH MINISTRY: A COMPREHENSIVE APPROACH

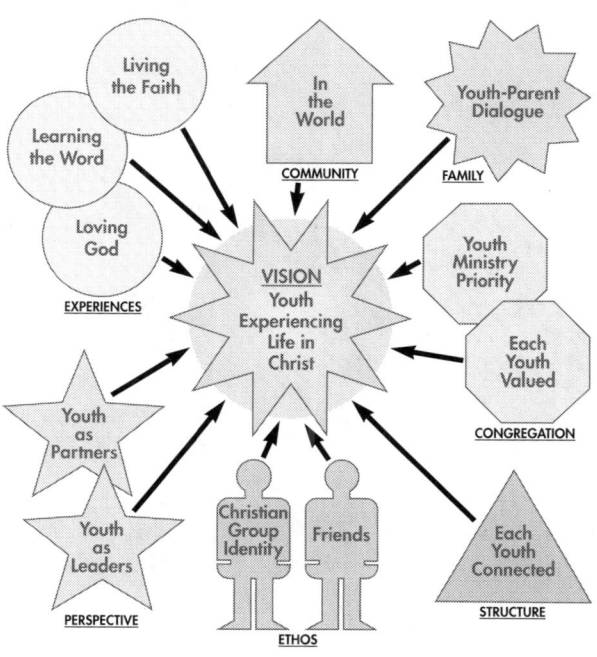

The Big Picture

FAMILY

Research is clear that **parent-youth dialogue** about matters of faith is crucial for youth to develop mature faith. Youth themselves express desire to be listened to, to have boundaries, and to have parental involvement in their lives. Parents need skills for relating to their changing teens as well as assurance that their values and voice do matter to their youth. How do we in the church facilitate parent-youth dialogue?

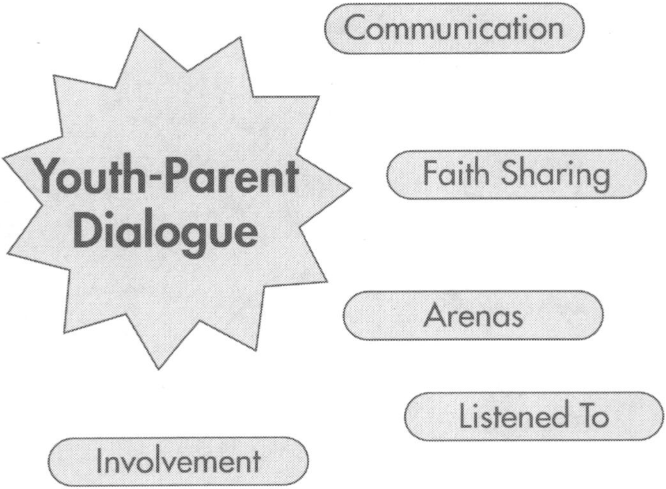

Youth-Parent Dialogue

- Communication
- Faith Sharing
- Arenas
- Listened To
- Involvement

How to Use Music With Youth

CONGREGATION

Youth ministry is the ministry of the whole congregation, beginning with making **youth ministry a priority**: prayer for the ministry, people (not just one person), time, effort, training, resources, and funding. The goal for the congregation is **each youth valued**. Interaction with adults, including mentors, positive language about youth, prayer partners for each one, simply being paid attention to—these are active roles for the congregation.

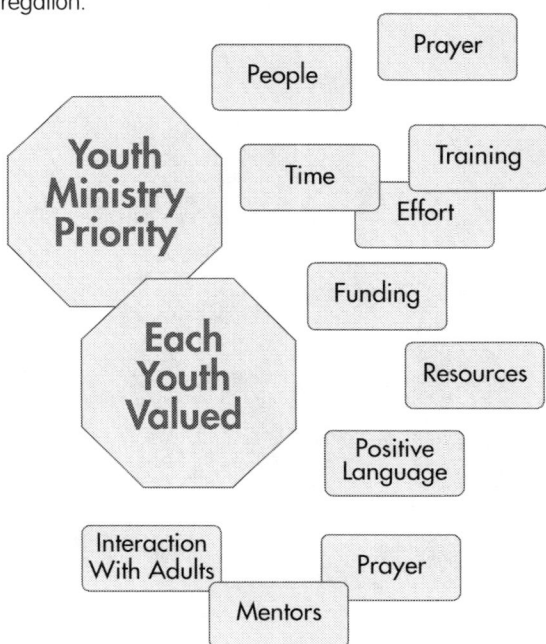

The Big Picture

STRUCTURE

Whatever shape the ministry takes, the goal is to have **each youth connected**. Sunday school and youth group are only a beginning. What are the needs of the youth? What groups (even of only 2 or 3 youth) and what times would help connect young people to the faith community? How easy is it for new youth to enter? How well do we stay in touch with the changing needs of our youth? Do we have structures in place that facilitate communication? outreach? "How" can vary; it's the "why" that's crucial.

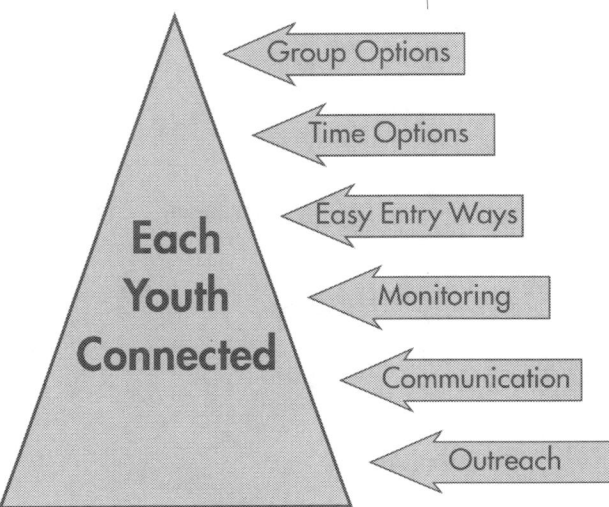

ETHOS

We are relational beings; we all need **friends**. The support, caring, and accountability friends provide help youth experience the love of God. As those friendships are nurtured within **Christian group identity**, young people claim for themselves a personal identity of being Christian. What language, rituals, traditions, and bonding experiences mark each grouping within the youth ministry as distinctively Christian?

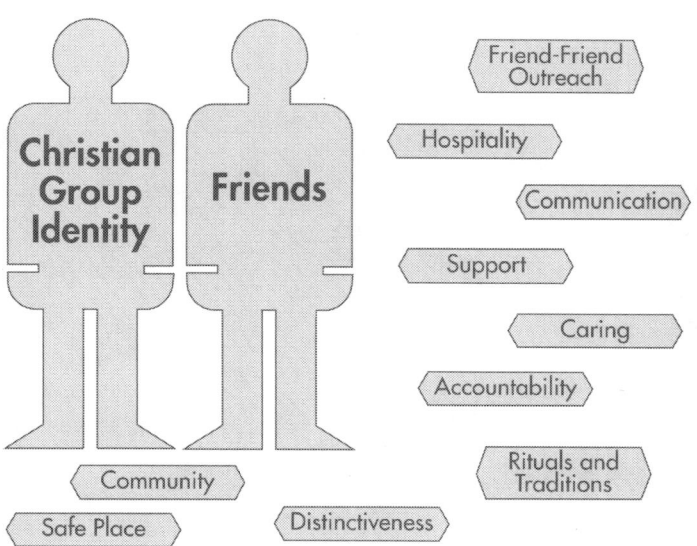

The Big Picture

PERSPECTIVE

The Big Picture

Youth are keenly aware of being seen as problems, being treated as objects to be fixed, or as recipients too inexperienced to have anything to offer. What would happen if we operated from the perspective of seeing **youth as leaders, youth as partners**? We would listen to them more, be intentional about identifying their gifts, take seriously their input, encourage their decision making, and train them for leadership roles.

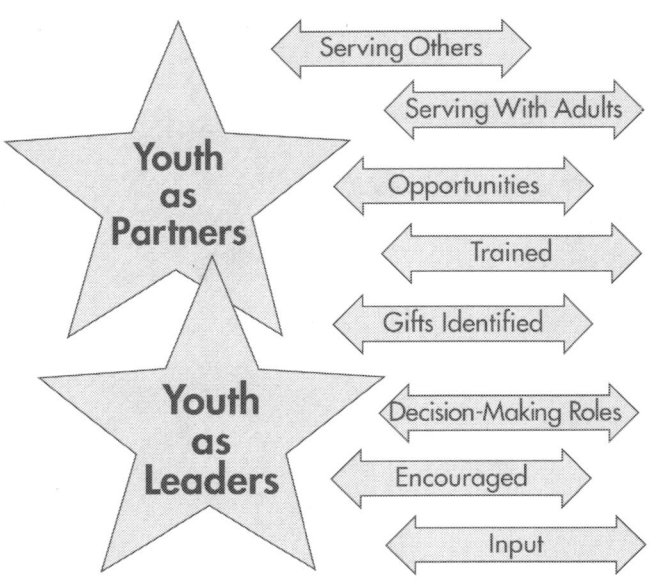

Youth as Partners
- Serving Others
- Serving With Adults
- Opportunities
- Trained
- Gifts Identified

Youth as Leaders
- Decision-Making Roles
- Encouraged
- Input

EXPERIENCES

Worship, devotions, prayer, and participation in the community of faith build for youth the experience of **loving God**. Study and reflection upon the Bible and the faith are crucial for **learning the Word**. Being among people who are Christian role models and grappling with difficult moral, ethical, justice, and stewardship issues help young people with **living the faith**. Curriculum resources specifically provide material to facilitate these three kinds of experiences.

The Big Picture

The Big Picture

COMMUNITY

As Christians, youth are challenged to be **in the world** as servants, as witnesses, as leaven—making a difference with their lives, giving others a glimpse of the Kingdom. What opportunities, what training, what support do we give youth to equip them for ministry beyond the walls of the church building?

Serving

Witnessing

Leaven/Salt/Light